W9-DHF-882

Money Business

Banks and Banking

ERNESTINE GIESECKE

Heinemann Library
Chicago, Illinois

© 2003 Reed Educational & Professional Publishing
Published by Heinemann Library,
an imprint of Reed Educational & Professional Publishing,
Chicago, Illinois

Customer Service 888-454-2279
Visit our website at www.heinemannlibrary.com

All rights reserved. No part of this publication may be
reproduced or transmitted in any form or by any means,
electronic or mechanical, including photocopying, recording,
taping, or any information storage and retrieval system,
without permission in writing from the publisher.

Designed by Herman Adler Design
Printed and bound in the United States by Lake Book
Manufacturing, Inc.

07 06 05 04 03
10 9 8 7 6 5 4 3 2 1

Library of Congress Cataloging-in-Publication Data
Giesecke, Ernestine, 1945-
   Money business : banks & banking / Ernestine Giesecke.
      v. cm. — (Everyday economics)
Includes bibliographical references and index.
Contents: Banks — Early banking — Types of banks —
Central banks —The history of U.S. banking — The U.S.
Central Bank — Banks and the economy — Banking services
— Choosing a bank — Banking around the world — Careers
in banking — Keeping track of money.
   ISBN 1-58810-490-7 (HC), 1-58810-953-4 (Pbk.)
   1. Banks and banking—Juvenile literature. [1. Banks and
banking.] I. Title.
HG1609 .G542 2002
332.1—dc21
                                   2002000804

Acknowledgments
The author and publisher are grateful to the following for
permission to reproduce copyright material:
Cover photographs by (L) Phil Banko/Stone/Getty Images,
(R) Eyewire Collection, and (Bck) Andrew Ward/Life
File/PhotoDisc
pp. 2, 3T Corbis; pp. 3B, 5B, 33, 37, 39 PhotoDisc; pp. 4
Panos Pictures; pp. 5T, 25B, 31 Spencer Grant/PhotoEdit,
Inc.; p. 7 Giraudon/Art Resource, NY; pp. 8, 15B Peter
Newark's American Pictures; pp. 9, 14R, 17, 18, 42
Bettmann/Corbis; pp. 10, 24T, 29 Tony Freeman/PhotoEdit,
Inc.; p. 11 Brown Brothers; pp. 12, 47, 48 Pawel
Libera/Corbis; p. 13 Hulton Pictures/Getty Images; p. 14L
Francis G. Mayer/Corbis; p. 15T 2001 American
Numismatic Society; p. 16 Mary Evans Picture Library; p. 20
Paul Conklin/PhotoEdit, Inc.; pp. 24, 28 Michael
Brosilow/Heinemann Library; pp. 25T, 32 Jeff
Greenberg/Visuals Unlimited; p. 27 Stock Montage; p. 34
Bill Wisser; p. 35 Hulton-Deutsch Collection/Corbis; p. 38
Doranne Jacobson; p. 40, 43 David Young-Wolff/PhotoEdit,
Inc.; p. 41 Still Pictures/Peter Arnold, Inc.
Illustration on page 33 provided by Carol Stutz

Every effort has been made to contact copyright holders of
any material reproduced in this book. Any omissions will be
rectified in subsequent printings if notice is given to the
publisher.

332.1
GIE
i-03
1357768

Note to the Reader: Some words are shown in
bold, **like this.** You can find out what they mean
by looking in the glossary.

Contents

Banks

Banks are businesses that specialize in providing **services** dealing with money. One thing a bank does is accept people's **deposits.** Deposits are money that the bank's customers put in the bank for safekeeping. When they make a deposit, customers trust that they will be able to take their money out of the bank whenever they want to, or at a specific future date. Most people place their money in banks for two reasons. First, banks offer a safe place to keep money. Second, banks pay their customers for depositing money in the bank. This payment is called **interest.**

Know It

People who deposit money in a bank are actually lending it to the bank. The bank usually pays interest for the use of the **funds.**

Customers can choose from a variety of services offered at local, state, and national banks. A customer often has to pay for these services with interest charges, fees, or **penalties.**

On average, banks earn an amount about equal to one percent of their assets—**loans** and **investments**—every year.

Modern banks offer a variety of services including: safeguarding deposits, paying interest on deposits, providing a means of payment, providing credit cards and debit cards, making loans, and offering electronic banking.

The bank uses the deposits it receives to make loans. A loan is money lent out to a **borrower.** The bank charges the borrower for the use of the money. This charge is also called interest.

Individuals and businesses borrow from banks. People may borrow the money they need to buy a home or a new car. Companies borrow money to buy equipment and build new factories. By lending money, banks help make the production of **goods** and services easier. In an indirect way, they help create jobs.

Like all businesses, banks try to earn **profits.** Banks earn profits when the interest they collect from borrowers is more than the interest they pay to customers. Banks also earn profits through fees they charge. For example, banks often collect fees for customer services such as offering checking accounts, selling insurance, and keeping track of loans. Banks can also earn profits by making wise investments.

Bank buildings, like the one pictured here, are often built to show strength and success. Banks want their customers to feel confident that the money they deposit will be safe.

Bank Profits

Interest Charged
− Interest Paid
+ Service Fees
+ Profits from Investments
Bank Profits

Early Banking

Banking is one of civilization's oldest occupations. In ancient Greece and Rome, people who acted as bankers had their stands or tables in the marketplaces. The first mention of bankers conducting business near the Roman Forum occurs in about 350 B.C.E. Their main job was to change money—exchanging foreign coins for Greek or Roman coins. For a fee, these bankers often managed the money-related affairs of others and accepted **deposits** from customers. The bankers then made a **profit** by lending the money to other customers. Sometimes a banker would lend money without having proof that it could be repaid. In a case like this, the banker lost everything he owned.

During the Middle Ages, Muslim **merchants** developed a bill of exchange to make trading easier. A bill of exchange is a way to **transfer** money from one location to another.

For example, a merchant in Athens might plan to spend a specific amount of money for goods in China. The merchant could deposit that amount of money with a banker in Athens. The Athenian banker would then write, or draw up, a bill

Good book

The books of Roman bankers were highly respected for their accuracy, especially with regard to dates. This allowed bankers' books to be used in courts of law as unshakable evidence.

Know It

The word bank comes from the Italian word *banco*, meaning "bench." Early Italian bankers conducted their business on benches in streets or marketplaces.

Bills of exchange allowed people to pay out money without having the actual cash in hand.

City A
Merchant A →
bill of exchange
pay Merchant B
20 gold pieces
→ **City B**
Banker
pays 20 gold pieces on behalf of Merchant A
↓
Merchant B

of exchange payable to the merchant. When the Athenian merchant took the bill of exchange to China, he could use it to pay for goods. This method of payment meant a merchant did not have to carry bags of heavy gold coins or worry about being robbed on a long and dangerous trip.

More modern banking began to develop during the 1200s, mainly in Italy at first. Italian cities that were heavily involved in trade—such as Florence, Rome, and Venice—became home to large banking firms. Slowly, banking spread to other Italian cities, and then throughout Europe. By the 1600s, London bankers were providing **services** similar to those provided by modern banks.

The following is part of an official **loan** contract drawn up in Genoa, Italy in 1161. The banker was Salvo of Piacenza. The **borrower** was Embrone, who borrowed £100. The amount to repay was £120.

*"I, Embrone, have taken in loan from you, Salvo of Piacenza, £100 Genoese, for which I shall pay you or your messenger ... £120 within one year; but if I wish to pay you the aforesaid £100 and accrued **interest** before the next Feast of Purification, you must accept them."*

The Feast of the Purification occurs on February 2.

Bankers were rarely from wealthy families, yet they were able to gather considerable wealth. This painting shows a prosperous banker and his assistants at work in the fifteenth century.

Types of Banks

Today the term "bank" is often used to identify a variety of **financial institutions.** In general, there are two types of banks: commercial banks and central banks.

A commercial bank is a business owned by the people who **invest** in it. These people, called investors, expect the bank to make a **profit.** The investors share the bank's profit.

In the United States, a commercial bank must have a bank charter in order to operate. A bank charter is a document that gives the bank the government's permission to operate. There are two types of charters: **federal** charters and state charters.

According to the signs in the drawing on this bank in Hackensack, New Jersey, it was acting as a national bank as well as a savings bank.

A bank with a federal charter is a national bank. Such a bank is allowed to include the word "national" in its name. For example, both the First National Bank of New England and Wilbur National have federal charters. A bank without a federal charter may not use the word "national" in its name.

Know It

The Office of the Comptroller of the Currency supervises more than 2,200 national banks and 56 federal branches of foreign banks in the U.S. today.

National banks belong to a system that makes and **enforces** rules for operating banks. The Office of the Comptroller of the Currency, an agent of the U.S. Department of the Treasury, is responsible for supervising national banks.

Commercial banks accept **deposits** and make **loans** to individuals and businesses. In addition, they accept on-demand deposits—deposits that can be **withdrawn** at any time, without notice. Money in a checking account is an example of an on-demand deposit. Today's commercial banks also offer **services** such as safe deposit boxes, **investment** management, and trust services.

Other banks have state charters. Such banks may or may not have the word "state" in their names. For example, both the Bank of Quincy and the Shawnee State Bank are chartered by the state of Illinois. Each is supervised by that state's Office of Banking and Real Estate. Every state has an agency that oversees banks in that state.

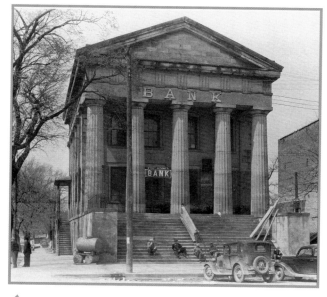

Even the buildings of small-town banks, like this bank in Shawneston, Illinois, were designed to look stable and make people feel confident in them.

When you think of a "bank," you might include institutions such as savings banks, savings and loan associations, and credit unions. These businesses are not really banks. Usually, they do not offer all the **services** available at commercial banks.

Know It

Savings banks, savings and loan associations, and credit unions are often called "thrifts" because their main goal is to encourage saving.

Originally, the goal of savings banks was to provide a safe place for poor working people to save for their retirement. A group of people called a board of trustees made business decisions for the bank. Most of the banks were mutual savings banks. This meant that the people who **deposited** money shared in any **profits** the bank made. Today, however, most saving banks are run by investors

At one time, savings and loans had names such as thrift and loan associations, cooperative banks, and homestead associations.

Savings and loan associations are most often found in the northeastern United States. The first savings and loan association in the United States opened in Pennsylvania in 1831.

who share in the bank's profits themselves. Investors elect a board of directors to make the bank's business decisions. Savings banks specialize in giving **loans** for buying homes.

Savings and loan associations are another type of **financial institution.** In the past, most of the loans made by savings and loans paid for building, buying, or remodeling homes. Today, savings and loan associations offer a wide range of services, including loans to businesses as well as individuals. Some savings and loan associations are mutual institutions. Just as with mutual savings banks, the depositors share in the profits of a mutual savings and loan. If a savings and loan is owned by investors, then investors share in the institution's profits. Most savings and loans operate with **federal** charters.

A credit union is a financial institution formed by people with something in common. For example, all the members of a credit union may work for the same company, or they may all belong to the same church. The credit union accepts deposits from its members and makes loans to its members. The members of a credit union share in its profits.

Ration coupons

During World War II, items such as sugar, coffee, meat, gasoline, and fuel oil were in short supply. Banks gave out coupons, called ration coupons, that allowed people to buy small amounts of these hard-to-get products.

Central Banks

A central bank is usually a government agency. Even though these agencies are called banks, they do not accept **deposits** from or lend money to individuals. Central banks have different responsibilities in different countries.

The first responsibility of most central banks is to make sure that the commercial banking system is safe and healthy. To do this, central banks make and **enforce** the rules that commercial banks must follow.

Most central banks work closely with their governments to keep their country's **economy** healthy. In a healthy economy, the **interest** rates, prices, and overall economic activity are stable—in other words, the value of the country's money is stable. To keep the value of money stable, central banks control the money supply. The money supply is made up of all the money in a country, including cash and money deposited in banks. In the United States, the **Federal** Reserve System regulates the money supply, making sure that the value of U.S. currency does not change significantly.

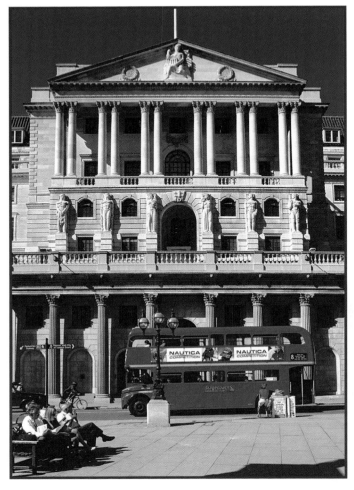

The Bank of England is the central bank of the United Kingdom. It was founded in 1694 to act as the government's banker and **debt**-manager after it received a **loan** of over one million pounds.

Money Supply = Cash + Bank Deposits
(All money in a country)

Nearly all central banks act as bankers for governments, taking in deposits and making loans to the government. In an emergency, a central bank can lend money to a commercial bank that needs cash to meet the demands of unexpected **withdrawals.** In this case, the central bank acts as a "lender of last resort." Banks that borrow money from the central bank are expected to repay the loans as quickly as possible.

Know It

Sometimes prices are not stable, but keep rising. This effect is called inflation. When inflation occurs, the dollar you spend on a loaf of bread one week may buy only a half a loaf six weeks later.

So much money. . .so little value

In the 1920s, inflation in Germany was so bad that it took boxes of **bank notes** just to buy bread. In fact, small purchases took so many bank notes that stores collected them in boxes and cartons instead of cash registers.

The History of U.S. Banking

After the **Revolutionary War,** the United States worked to set up its own **economic** and **financial** systems. One group of Americans felt that an **industrial** economy would need large banks. They also felt that the **federal** government should be responsible for supervising banks. A second group thought that large banks would not be needed because the country would remain a nation of farms. They felt that the states should be responsible for supervising banks.

Congress established the first Bank of the United States in 1791. This bank acted as both a commercial bank and a central bank. It made **loans,** safeguarded **deposits,** issued **currency,** and watched over the practices of state banks. The first bank worked well. Even so, many individuals, businesses, and state banks felt that the bank had too much power. They pressured Congress not to renew the bank's charter in 1811.

Thomas Jefferson

Know It

Two members of President George Washington's administration were among those who disagreed about banks. Alexander Hamilton, Secretary of the Treasury, was in favor of large banks. Thomas Jefferson, Secretary of State, was against large banks.

Alexander Hamilton

After the first bank closed, the number of state banks grew quickly. Many of these banks issued great numbers of **bank notes** even though they did not have enough gold and silver coins on hand to exchange for the notes. These banks failed.

Once again, Congress set up a central bank to watch over state banks. But, like the first bank, people felt the second Bank of the United States had too much power—so Congress did not renew its charter either.

When the second national bank closed in 1836, banking in the United States developed many problems. The uneven money supply led to great changes in prices. Banks made risky loans, lost money, and could not pay depositors. **Counterfeit** bank notes were easy to make and became a widespread problem, as people could make the money they needed.

Banks in frontier towns offered a safe place to store cash and gold. However, they also made many risky loans. This practice made these banks more likely to fail.

Unique cash

In the early part of our country's history, each bank issued its own bank notes. A customer could exchange a note for gold or silver at any time.

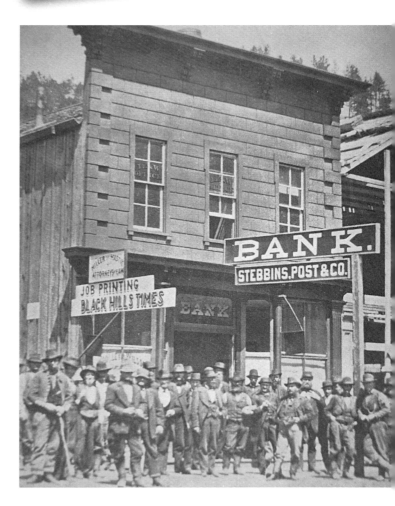

In 1863 and 1864, Congress moved to establish a national banking system. This system was designed to control the number of **bank notes in circulation.** However, even with the controls, there was not always enough cash, and once again, many banks failed because they did not have enough money available for their customers' **withdrawals.**

The **Federal** Reserve Act of 1913 created the Federal Reserve System, often called "the Fed." To make sure the Fed did not have too much power, Congress created twelve Federal Reserve Banks scattered throughout the country. A board of governors in Washington, D.C. helps to oversee the system.

Beginning in 1929, the **economies** of the world experienced serious problems. In October the stock market crashed, leading many businesses, as well as farms, to fail. People could not repay the money they borrowed from banks. Banks could not meet their customers' demands for withdrawals. Thousands of banks failed.

Bankrupt banks

In 1929, 25,000 banks operated in the United States. By 1933, 7,200 of them—or one in three—had failed and closed their doors for good.

This drawing shows the inside of a bank in the early 1900s. The bank cashiers behind the bars counted out the amount of money they took in or gave out. Eventually they came to be known as "tellers."

Know It

From 1929 to 1939, much of the Western world experienced great **financial** losses. In United States history, this time is called the Great Depression. Thousands of businesses, farms, and banks failed during this time.

President Franklin Roosevelt signed the Federal Reserve Act of 1933, creating the Federal Deposit Insurance Corporation (FDIC).

In 1933, Congress again addressed the nation's banking problems. It created the Federal **Deposit** Insurance Corporation (FDIC). Congress designed the FDIC to insure bank deposits and to reduce the number of risky **loans** banks made. At about the same time, Congress created the Federal Savings and Loan Insurance Corporation (FSLIC) to insure deposits at savings and loans.

Fifty years later, in the 1980s, more than a thousand savings and loan institutions failed. Many of them suffered from poor supervision and management. Outright **fraud** and large numbers of high-risk loans also contributed to the failures. So many

Savings and Loan crisis

When the FSLIC went bankrupt, taxpayers had to bear the financial burden. The crisis ended up costing taxpayers an estimated $350 billion—more than $4,000 for each man, woman, and child in the nation.

savings and loans failed that the FSLIC went **bankrupt.** Congress acted to make the FDIC responsible for insuring savings and loans. It also made laws creating stronger controls over the business practices of savings and loans. Later, the Savings Association Insurance Fund (SAIF) was created. The SAIF is now responsible for insuring savings and loans.

The U.S. Central Bank

The **Federal** Reserve System, or "the Fed," is the central bank for the United States. The Fed consists of twelve Federal Reserve Banks, each operating in one of the country's twelve Federal Reserve districts. Most districts also have Federal Reserve Bank branches. There are 25 branch banks in all. Each branch bank offers many of the same **services** offered by the main banks.

The work of the Fed is directed by two groups of people. The board of governors manages the system. The board has seven members, each appointed by the president of the United States and approved by the Senate. Members serve for fourteen years. The president names one member to chair, or lead, the board for four years at a time. The chairperson may serve for more than one term.

The second group of people who direct the Fed form the Federal Open Market Committee. This committee sets the **monetary** policy of the United States. The committee is made up of the members of the board of governors, as well as the president of the New York City Federal Reserve Bank, and the presidents of four other Federal Reserve Banks from around the country.

Another group that advises the Fed is the Federal Advisory Council. They do

Know It

About 4,000 banks are members of the Fed. This is less than half the number of banks in the country. However, these banks hold about three-quarters of the country's **deposits.**

Alan Greenspan was first appointed chairperson of the Fed in 1987. His current term expires in 2004. Greenspan also chairs the Federal Open Market Committee.

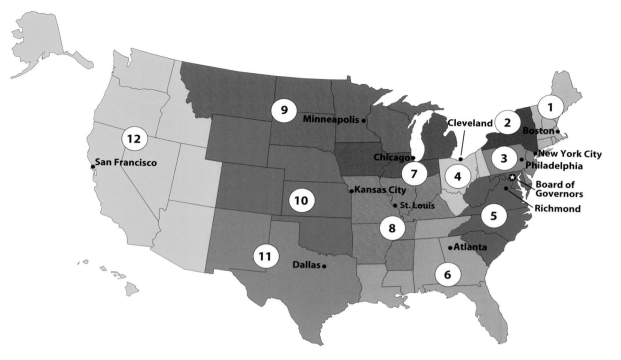

The Federal Reserve System has twelve districts located in different regions of the United States.

not help direct the Fed, but offer advise on issues when called upon. The council consists of twelve members, one of whom is elected by the board of directors of the twelve Federal Reserve districts.

The Fed reports to Congress about the policies it proposes. However, the Fed is free to make its own policy decisions. Also, although the Fed is a government agency, it does not get money from the government. The Fed earns money from its **investments** and from the fees it charges banks for its services. However, the Fed does not pay **interest** on the deposits it accepts from banks.

The Fed's responsibilities include conducting the nation's monetary policy, supervising and regulating banking institutions, maintaining the stability of the **financial** system, and providing financial services for the government.

The Fed's most important job is to help manage the nation's **economy.** To do this, the Fed encourages economic growth and controls inflation. The Fed sets the interest rates that determine the cost of borrowing money. By controlling interest rates, the Fed controls how much money is in **circulation** as well as how easy it is to get **loans.** The way the Fed influences interest rates is part of its monetary policy.

The Federal Reserve System, or "the Fed," has been the foundation of American banking and economy since 1913. The system has its main offices in Washington, D.C.

Another job of the Fed centers on making and **enforcing** rules banks must follow. Because banks conduct most of their business with "other people's" money, the nation's **economy** suffers when banks operate recklessly. This means that each bank's health and stability is important to everyone, not just the to bank's **investors** and customers. Bankers can make many of a bank's day-to-day decisions. But every institution that takes **deposits**—whether it's a member of the **Federal** Reserve System or not—must follow the rules about how much of its deposits it may lend.

Banks in the Federal Reserve System use the Federal Reserve Banks in many of the same ways that people use banks.

The Fed provides several **services** involving the **transfer** of money. One such service is to act as a clearinghouse for processing checks. A clearinghouse allows banks to accept checks and make payments to one another using the smallest possible exchange of **funds.**

Here is an example of how a clearinghouse works. Suppose you have a checking account at AcmeBank of Missouri and you write a check for $50 at a music store. The music store deposits the $50 check in its account at MegaBank of New York. At the same time, the music store sends a $250 check to the electric company. The electric company deposits the $250 check in its account at AcmeBank. Each bank sends the checks that were deposited to the clearinghouse.

How a Clearinghouse Works

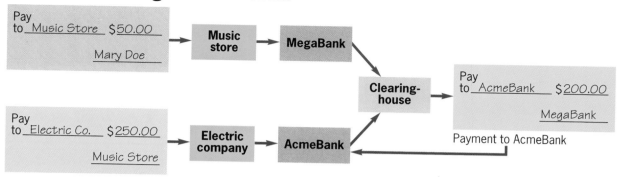

The clearinghouse sorts and examines all the checks. It determines that AcmeBank needs to pay $50 to MegaBank, and MegaBank needs to pay $250 to AcmeBank. The payments can be made at the same time if MegaBank pays $200 to AcmeBank. The Fed, acting as a clearinghouse, may process millions of checks in one day. As a result, the amount of money that needs to be transferred is as small as possible.

The Fed also offers electronic transfer services. These services transfer money without cash or checks actually going anywhere. For example, the Fed's Automated Clearing House (ACH) deals with automatic deposits such as paychecks and **Social Security** checks. The ACH also handles automatic payments for bills such as telephone bills, car payments, rent, or house payments. The customer agrees to have the amount of each bill automatically **withdrawn** from his or her checking account. The ACH makes certain that the payments are the correct amounts and are delivered on time.

These are the letters and numbers used to indicate the Federal Reserve Banks.		
Boston, MA	A	1
New York, NY	B	2
Philadelphia, PA	C	3
Cleveland, OH	D	4
Richmond, VA	E	5
Atlanta, GA	F	6
Chicago, IL	G	7
St. Louis, MO	H	8
Minneapolis, MN	I	9
Kansas City, KS	J	10
Dallas, TX	K	11
San Francisco, CA	L	12

Know It

Fedwire is a service offered by the Fed and used by banks and other **financial institutions.** Fedwire allows banks to safely transfer enormous amounts of money. In 2000, the Fed processed more than 100 million Fedwire transfers, averaging about $3.5 million each.

Banks and the Economy

Banks are the main place consumers can get **loans** for items such as cars, houses, and education. Banks are also the main lenders to businesses. When they make loans, banks have the power to create money.

A bank does not lend out all the **deposits** it receives—it must keep some money in reserve. The Fed decides what percentage of a bank's deposits the bank must keep in reserve. After it sets aside its reserve requirement, the rest of the money a bank has on hand is its excess.

Suppose the Fed requires banks to set aside ten percent of their money for reserve. Banks use the excess to create money in the following way: when you deposit $1,000 in YourBank, YourBank sets aside ten percent, or $100, as its reserve.

YourBank can now lend the other $900 to Bea Sweet to open a bakery. Ms. Sweet deposits the $900 in her account at HerBank. HerBank sets aside $90 as its reserve.

In the summer of 2001, **federal** regulators closed a Chicago-area savings and loan. The institution had suffered huge losses by making loans to high-risk **borrowers.** The regulators found that the bank had lost nearly all its money and **investments.** The failure is expected to cost the FDIC about $500 million, making it one of the costliest failures ever of a United States **financial institution.**

Next, HerBank lends $810 to Larry Moore to buy a car. Mr. Moore pays the $810 to WeBeCars. WeBeCars deposits the $810 at TheirBank. TheirBank sets aside $81 as its reserve. TheirBank can now lend the other $729 as its own excess reserves, continuing the pattern. In this example, your original $1,000 has become $2,710 ($1000 + $900 + $810) in deposits in three different banks! Each time the excess is lent out and deposited somewhere else, more money is "created."

The Fed can encourage banks to create more money by lowering the percentage of deposits banks must keep in reserve. This means there will be more money available to lend. The Fed can encourage banks to create less money by raising the percentage that banks must hold in reserve. If there is a sharp increase in bank reserves, the amount available for lending decreases. This can lead to a situation called a "credit crunch." Changing lending patterns is one way the Fed controls the nation's **economy.**

Know It

Creating money is not the same as printing money or issuing money. Only the U.S. Mint can print money, only the Fed can issue money, and only banks can create money, as they exchange it during the lending process.

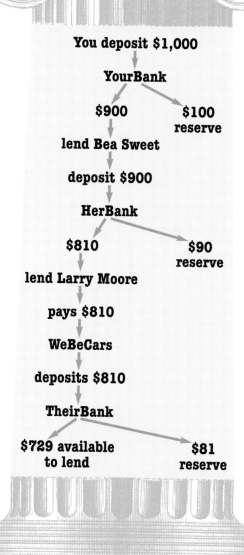

Multiplier Effect

You deposit $1,000

YourBank

$900 → $100 reserve

lend Bea Sweet

deposit $900

HerBank

$810 → $90 reserve

lend Larry Moore

pays $810

WeBeCars

deposits $810

TheirBank

$729 available to lend → $81 reserve

Money Availability
Lower reserves = more money for loans
Higher reserves = less money for loans

Banking Services

Banks safeguard, or keep safe, the **deposits** placed in their care. They keep cash available for people to **withdraw** when they need it, and they have insurance to cover any losses from robberies. More importantly, government-sponsored programs insure the money that people deposit in banks.

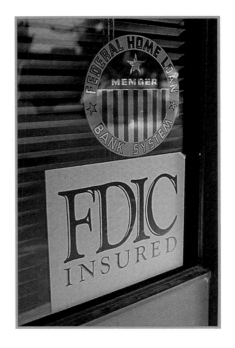

In the United States, the **Federal** Deposit Insurance Corporation (FDIC) insures deposits in nearly all the country's commercial and savings banks. The FDIC also administers the Savings Association Insurance Fund (SAIF), to insure deposits in savings and loan institutions. If a credit union has a federal charter, the National Credit Union Share Insurance Fund insures its accounts. Each of these agencies insures savings accounts up to a maximum balance of $100,000.

One of the most common forms of deposit is the passbook savings account. A passbook is a book for recording every deposit and withdrawal. A passbook account usually earns a low rate called **minimum interest.** The customer can withdraw any or all of his

Know It

To open a passbook savings account or obtain CDs, most banks require that you give two forms of identification and a **Social Security** number.

or her money without giving the bank advance notice. The minimum amount needed to open a passbook savings account is often about $100 to $200.

Some banks offer "time deposits," savings accounts held for a fixed length of time. A customer with a time deposit account must give the bank notice before withdrawing any money. There is often a **penalty** for withdrawing money before the end of the fixed time period. Banks offer time deposits as certificates of deposit, or CDs. The interest paid for a CD is usually more than the interest for passbook savings, and longer-term CDs earn more than those held for a shorter time. CDs are often available for a variety of terms, such as six months, one year, or three years. The minimum deposit for a CD may be $1,000 to $2,500.

CERTIFICATES OF DEPOSIT
WEEK OF 10 24
$ 1000 MIN. DEPOSIT

	RATE	ANNUAL YIELD
3 MONTHS	2.60%	2.63%
6 MONTHS	3.20%	3.25%
1 YEAR	3.94%	4.00%
18 MONTHS	4.67%	4.75%
2 YEARS	4.67%	4.75%
30 MONTH	4.67%	4.75%
3 YEARS	4.67%	4.75%
MONEY MARKET		2.50%

IRA
	RATE	YIELD
18 MOS	3 85	3 91
24 & 30 36 MOS	4 45	4 52
	4 45	4 52

The interest rates for CDs can change every week. Most banks post the interest rates for CDs in their lobby.

A safe place

Banks often share their vault space with individuals who rent safe deposit boxes. Anything placed in a safe deposit box is as safe as the money in the bank's vault. The box is a safe place to keep valuable coin collections, expensive jewelry, and important papers. However, any money placed in the safe deposit box does not earn interest.

A bank may grant a **loan** to a customer if the bank thinks the customer will be able to repay the loan. For most loans, the **borrower** is required to provide collateral, something of value that the bank can take if the borrower does not repay the loan.

Most loans must be paid back within a specific time limit. The borrower usually must make regular payments, often monthly. The **interest** charged for loans varies from less than one percent to more than twenty percent. The loan agreement must clearly state the **annual** interest rate—also called the annual percentage rate (APR)—as well as the total amount of interest to be paid. In addition, the agreement must specify the total cost of the loan, including any fees or other charges.

Compare the information needed for this loan agreement with the information found in the medieval loan agreement from 1161 on page 7.

Amount of loan

Annual percentage rate

Amount of monthly payments

Total amount to be repaid

Loan fees

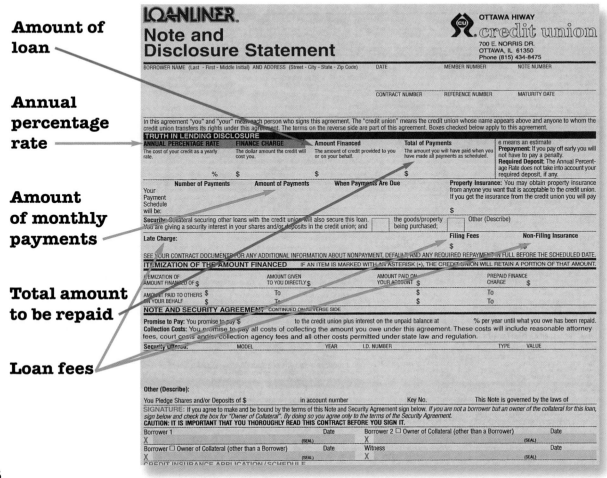

A personal, or character, loan is based on the borrower's personal credit history and sometimes on their character. These loans may be made without collateral. With a new car loan, for example, the collateral is the car itself. If the borrower fails to repay the loan, the car will be **repossessed.**

Know It

A bank may not refuse a loan because of a borrower's race, religion, ethnic origin, or gender. A bank may, however, require that a borrower also be a depositor of the bank. Loans from a credit union are made only to members of the credit union.

A **mortgage** is a loan to purchase real estate, such as a house or farm. With a mortgage, the borrower pledges the property as collateral. That is, the lender can take the property if the borrower fails to repay the loan.

War bonds

During World War I and World War II, banks offered war bonds for sale. When a person bought a war bond, he or she was lending money to the government to help pay for the war. The loan was for ten years. A bond that cost $75 when it was purchased could be redeemed ten years later for $100.

To Have and to Hold!

WAR BONDS

Magill-Weinsheimer Company 6M 6-26-44 Chicago, Illinois

In addition to offering savings accounts and **loans,** most banks also offer a convenient way to make payments. The bank's customers can pay a bill by writing a check. A check is a written instruction to pay a specified amount of money to a certain person upon demand. The check gives the bank permission to take that specified amount of money out of the customer's checking account.

Customers must keep track of the checks they have written and know how much money is left in their account. Each **transaction** should be recorded in a small booklet called a check register. The amount of each check written is subtracted from the **balance; deposits** are added to the balance.

Once a month, the bank sends each customer a statement that lists the checks and deposits the bank has recorded for the account. The customer can then compare his or her own record with that of the bank. This process is called balancing the account.

Check entry in register

Deposit entry in register

Total amount of deposits on statement

Check listing on statement

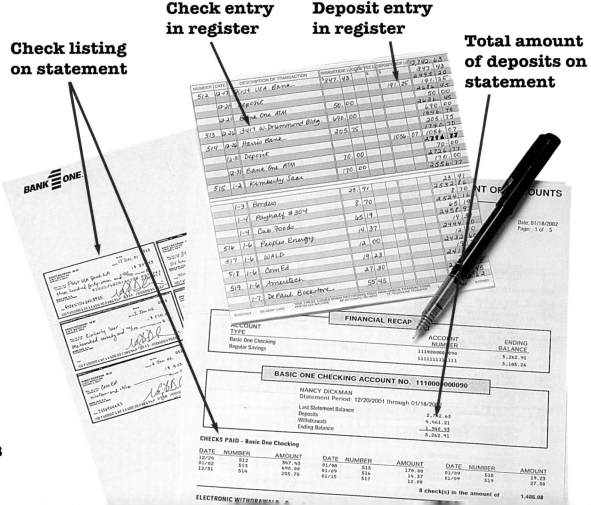

28

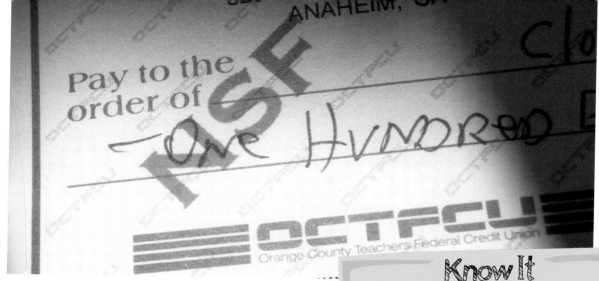

Minimum amounts for opening a checking account vary from about $100 to $1,000. There may be a certain amount of time a customer has to wait before writing checks from the newly opened account. Some checking accounts pay **interest,** while others may charge a fee.

In some cases, the customer's checking account might not have enough money to pay a check. When this happens, the check is returned, unpaid. The check will be marked NSF, meaning "not sufficient **funds.**" The fee charged for handling a returned check is about $20 to $30.

The bank can also issue a cashier's check for a small fee. This type of check cannot bounce because the customer pays the bank the dollar amount of the check. Then the bank is responsible for making the payment. Another form of guaranteed check is a certified check—one that the bank guarantees, or promises, to pay.

Know It

A check that is not payable due to insufficient funds "bounces back" to the person who wrote the check. This check may be described as a "bounced check" or "rubber check." Writing a check that you know will bounce is against the law.

In a recent year, banks earned about $6.2 million in bounced check fees. To avoid bounced check fees, make sure to:
- Always keep your checkbook balanced.
- Be sure there is money in your account before writing the next check.
- Learn the time it takes for the checks you deposit to "clear"—that is, find out how long it will be before the money is actually available in your account.

Many banks take advantage of today's computers and other electronic equipment to help customers make payments. For example, a customer may ask a bank to pay a regularly occurring bill, such as an electricity bill. The bank **withdraws** the amount of the bill from the customer's checking account and sends it to the electric company's bank account electronically.

Pay electronically

Paying bills automatically can be very convenient and save lots of time. However, the customer must be sure that there are **funds** available for the payments. Also, the customer must remember to record these payments in their check register.

Customers can also make payments using telephones and personal computers. The process is nearly the same. The customer asks the bank to take a specific amount of money from their checking account and **transfer** it to the appropriate business or individual.

HARDACKER INC.

AUTHORIZATION AGREEMENT FOR AUTOMATIC DEPOSITS OF PAYROLL CHECKS

I hereby authorize Hardacker Inc., hereinafter called Company, to initiate credit entries and/or adjust entries as may be from time to time required to my bank account(s) indicated below and further authorize the depository(ies) named below to credit and debit same to such account(s).

Bank Account #1 _____ Amount $_____

Name of Bank _____ Checking ____ Savings _____

City _____ State _____ Zip _____

Bank Transit/ABA # _____ Account #_____

This authority is to remain in full force and effect until Company has received written notification from me of its termination in such time and in such manner as to afford Company a reasonable opportunity to act on it.

Name _____ SSN _____

Signed _____ Date _____

Once an employee fills out a form like this, their company will automatically **deposit** the amount of their paycheck into the employee's account. Similar forms can be used to make automatic payments for **loans** and other bills.

When a customer uses a debit card, the amount of the purchase is instantly subtracted from their account.

In many stores, small computer **terminals** have replaced the cash registers. These terminals allow customers to pay for their purchases electronically before they leave the store. The customer does not need cash or checks, only a small plastic card called a debit card. As the customer **swipes** the card through the terminal's card reader, the **transaction** begins. The store's computers contact the customer's bank. The amount of the purchase is subtracted from the customer's checking account and transferred to the store's account.

Know It

The process that moves money from one account to another without using checks is called electronic funds transfer (EFT).

Wells Fargo Company provided telegraph communications to banks starting in 1864. In a way, one could say that that was the first electronic transaction. Today, Wells Fargo offers a wide variety of banking **services.**

The automated teller machine (ATM) is another electronic banking **service.** An ATM is a computer **terminal.** Customers can complete a variety of **transactions** at an ATM using a special card and a personal identification number (PIN). For example, customers can use an ATM to make **deposits, transfer funds** from one account to another, and **withdraw** limited amounts of cash. Banks have put ATMs at airports, in grocery stores, at sports stadiums, and in many other places. Because most ATMs operate day and night, every day of the year, they offer great convenience to a bank's customers.

ATMs are quick and easy to use. However, customers must remember to note all ATM transactions, as well as any fees, in their checking or savings account records.

Many banks offer credit cards that people can use to buy things. A customer's card is **swiped** through a terminal's card reader to make the transaction. Then the bank pays for the purchase directly. At the end of the month, the bank sends a statement to the customer, showing all the purchases made with the credit card for that month. The customer can choose to pay the entire amount or only part of it. If the customer pays only part of the amount due, he or she must also pay a finance charge, or **interest,** on the card's unpaid **balance.**

The newest electronic banking item is a smart card. This small plastic card, the size of a credit card, contains one or more computer chips. The card can be programmed for a specific amount of money, either **withdrawn** from the customer's account or paid in cash when the card was purchased. Each time the customer buys something, the amount of the purchase is subtracted from the balance stored on the card. Smart cards can be used again and again—when the original balance has been used up, the customer can pay another amount of money to "refill" the card.

One common example of a smart card is a phone card, a plastic card programmed with a specific amount of money to be used for telephone calls.

Smart cards can be used in many ways. People use smart cards as a form of identification, as well as to pay for purchases, travel, and phone calls.

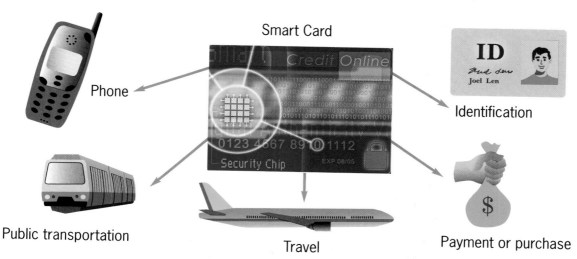

Smart Card

Phone

Identification

Public transportation

Travel

Payment or purchase

Choosing a Bank

There are many things to consider when choosing a bank. It is important to choose a bank with a good reputation. Many people choose a bank that is located close to home or work. Most people look for a bank that is open late some evenings so that they may use the bank after work.

Before opening a savings or checking account, a customer may want to find out what **services** and conveniences the bank offers. More importantly, a customer should learn about the cost of keeping a savings or checking account at a specific bank.

Know It

It is wise to find out the cost of doing business with a specific bank before depositing money at that bank.

Recent studies show that the average cost of having a bank checking account is about $200 a year.

Banking customers may visit several banks before choosing one to use. They should consider points such as location, business hours, and size.

Banks work hard to develop new ways of serving their customers. This drive-up banking window, among the first of its kind, opened in Hollywood, California, in 1951.

Most banks have fees even for savings accounts. For example, the bank might charge a fee of $12 a year if the account has a **balance** less than $100 and is not used for a year. A bank may charge $5 if the savings account is closed less than 90 days after it is opened. Some banks charge $5 to replace a lost passbook. Almost all banks charge a fee or **penalty** for cashing in CDs before the agreed due date.

Checking accounts can have a variety of fees associated with them as well. For example, opening a checking account at one bank may be free, but the bank may charge $0.15 to process each check. Another bank might charge between $3 and $10 a month for the account, but process checks for free. Many banks will offer free

Christmas club

In 1909, the Carlisle Trust Company in Carlisle, Pennsylvania offered the first Christmas savings club at a bank. Merkel Landis, the bank's treasurer, was responsible for the idea.

checking accounts if the account always stays above a specific **minimum** balance. The minimum balance to avoid fees can range from $250 at some banks to $1500 at other banks. Banks may even offer to pay **interest** on the money in a checking account if the customer maintains a minimum balance.

Bank customers need to be aware of the charges associated with using an ATM. Some banks charge a fee of $1 to $3 for using the bank's ATM. If a customer uses an ATM operated by a different bank, there may be another ATM charge, also ranging from $1 to $3. This means that if a customer makes a $20 **withdrawal** at an ATM not owned by the customer's bank, that withdrawal may cost as much as six dollars.

Know It

When you use an ATM, make sure you know if it is owned and operated by your bank or by a competing bank. The fees may be different for each type of ATM.

A customer should consider his or her banking habits when deciding what bank offers the best value. For example, she might be able to keep a **minimum balance** of $500 every month. She might write twelve checks a month, bounce one check a year, and use her bank's ATM for fifteen **transactions** a year. Using this information, a customer can compare the cost of banking at several banks, and choose the bank that best suits her needs.

Having to remember a PIN may soon be a thing of the past. It is possible that some ATMs will soon identify customers by a pattern in their eyes. This pattern is as unique as fingerprints.

Once you know what kind of bank account you want, make a list of the features, **services,** and costs of several banks.

Bank Features
Interest rate
FDIC membership
Minimum deposit
Limitations
Availability of funds

Bank Services
Direct deposit
ATM
Credit card
Debit card
Loans and mortgages
Deposit slips and other slips
Telephone assistance
Safe deposit box rental
Cashier's checks

Bank Costs
Maintenance
Low balance fee
ATM use
Returned check fee
Bounced check penalty
Check printing
Charge per check
Closed account fee

Using an ATM

To use an ATM, a customer **swipes** a small card into or through a card reader. The computer screen asks the customer to type in a personal identification number (PIN) to insure that the right person is using the card. Next, the customer chooses a **transaction—depositing,** withdrawing, or **transferring** money. Once the transaction is complete, the ATM prints a receipt showing the type and amount of the transaction.

Banking Around the World

The world's largest private banks have headquarters in Japan, Germany, Switzerland, the United Kingdom, and the United States. These private banks are owned by investors or corporations and operate in many countries throughout the world.

In Japan, large banks called city banks offer banking **services** to major **industrial** companies. Leading city banks include the Bank of Tokyo-Mitsubishi and the Sumitomo Bank. Smaller regional banks serve local businesses and smaller firms.

In many European countries, a few large banks, each with many branches, **dominate** the banking system. For example, in the United Kingdom, four large banks handle most of the nation's checking and credit **transactions.** Three banks dominate banking in Germany, while Swiss banking relies on two main banks.

Know It

The headquarters for some of the world's richest banks are located in various cities throughout Asia.

Swiss banks

Banks in Switzerland attract **deposits** from many countries because Swiss banks have a reputation for safety and secrecy.

Satellite communications and electronic banking mean that banks can serve customers in the farthest corners of the world—even in the middle of the desert.

United Kingdom

Unlike the Federal Reserve System, the Bank of England (the United Kingdom's central bank), does not regulate other banks. In the United Kingdom, the Financial Services Authority (FSA) regulates banks.

Banking in Canada also relies on a small number of commercial banks and their branches. Commercial banks in Canada are **federally** chartered and regulated.

Countries such as Algeria, Ethiopia, and Cuba do not allow private ownership of banks. Banks in these countries are nationalized, or under government control. Some Asian and South American countries have both national and private banks. For example, the government of India owns India's largest commercial banks, but there are hundreds of smaller private banks.

Until the late twentieth century, the Soviet Union and other **communist** nations had only national banks. After the Soviet Union broke apart in 1991, these countries reformed their banking systems, allowing private banks.

Although banks have a variety of electronics and technology to speed transactions, some tasks must still be done by hand. Here, a teller in a European currency exchange is counting **bank notes**.

The world's most expensive bank **fraud** centered on the Bank of Credit and Commerce International (BCCI). The bank was founded in 1972 and grew to about 400 branches worldwide. By the time its illegal activities were discovered (including money laundering), the bank had **debts** totaling twelve billion dollars owed to 150,000 depositors. BCCI shut down in mid-1991. By 1992, it was the largest scandal in banking history.

Countries with large Muslim populations, such as Egypt, have banks that operate according to religious rules. **Islam** prohibits Muslims from taking or paying **interest**. This is true no matter what the **loan** is for or what amount of interest is charged. As a result, Islamic banks make special arrangements with the people to whom they lend money. For example, the client may pay a fee for the loan, or the bank may receive a share of the **profits** in the client's business.

Know It

Banks around the world have begun to tailor the **services** they offer to meet the wide variety of customer needs.

Development banks offer **microcredit** to the poorest people, with loans for as little as $300. **Borrowers** use the money to buy materials they can use to produce something. For example, a borrower might buy cotton to weave fabric or materials to make bracelets. Microcredit loans are always for a year, and interest is fixed at twenty percent.

This Muslim couple is preparing to apply for a loan. They will not have to pay interest on the loan, opting instead to pay a fee.

Microcredit loans allow these poor women to buy the materials they need to weave baskets or to embroider quilts to earn money for their families.

Repayment starts in the second week of the loan and continues in small weekly payments. After the loan is repaid, the borrower may take out a new, larger loan. In addition to repaying the loan, each borrower has to start a saving plan to protect against disaster.

In addition to those in Pakistan, there are development, or trust, banks in countries such as India, Guatemala, the Dominican Republic, Russia, Colombia, and Zimbabwe.

The Grameen Bank of Pakistan is an example of a development bank. It has been in business for twenty years and is the largest rural bank in Bangladesh. Grameen has over two million borrowers and works in 35,000 villages throughout the country. The bank boasts that 99 percent of its loans are repaid.

Careers in Banking

A typical job in banking requires excellent skills for communication, sales, and working with people. A large number of jobs are as credit **analysts** and **loan** officers. A credit analyst reviews loan applications from businesses and individuals. Credit analysts can learn a lot about business as they look over the applications. A successful credit analyst pays attention to details and works well with customers.

Loan officers arrange complex loans to businesses and individuals. Loan officers usually have good selling skills and a solid understanding of how banking works. A loan officer position can lead to higher jobs within a bank.

Know It

In a 1992 survey of 100 jobs in the United States, banking ranked second in job satisfaction.

In the early part of the 1900s, women worked in banks, but only doing filing, and only in the bank's back rooms. Women were not allowed to be tellers or cashiers, or to work with customers.

In today's modern banks, teams of banking employees, including loan officers and customer service representatives, work together to make sure that the customer receives the best service possible.

Many bank managers begin their career as tellers or customer **service** representatives. People in these positions are responsible for helping customers with their banking business. Jobs like these require good people skills, dedication, and organization.

Other jobs in banking involve advertising, commercial card applications, personnel, operations, and communications. Banks employ many people who work with technology and computer applications.

Science in banking?

As odd as it sounds, even a scientist can find a career in banking! A person with scientific ability can work on some of the advanced products offered by the banks' **investment** divisions. A background in biology and technology can help a person figure out what firms are developing promising products in biotechnology.

Keeping Track of Money

Every person should be aware of how he or she saves and spends money. In addition, customers should keep detailed records of their **transactions** with banks. Then, when the customers receive their monthly bank statements, they should read them carefully. The customers' and the bank's records should both show the same transactions and **balances.**

Know It

Keeping clear and timely records of the money you spend and the money you receive is a good habit to develop early and keep practicing for life.

Statements from different banks may look slightly different from one another. However, all statements contain the same information about transactions. Every statement lists the following information: the name on the account, the account number, the date of the statement, and the beginning and ending date for the statement.

Most banks have **deposit** and **withdrawal** slips that a customer can use to make transactions while at their bank or while at an ATM.

Name **Date** **Account number** **Amount of deposit**

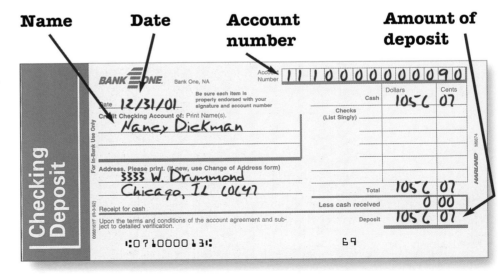

A statement for a savings account will give the dollar balance at the beginning date, the total amount of deposits, the total amount of withdrawals, any **interest** earned, and the dollar balance at the ending date.

> If you get hopelessly lost and feel there is no way to balance your account, go to the bank and ask for help. Ignoring the problem only makes you more likely to write checks that your account balance can't cover.

A statement for a checking account contains the same information. It also lists each check paid during the time covered by the statement.

On the back of most bank statements are directions on how to balance, or reconcile, the account. Errors should be reported to the bank as soon as possible. The bank statement should list the phone number and address necessary to ask questions or report an error.

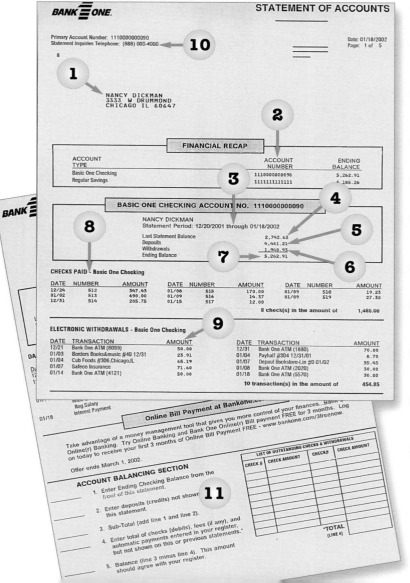

1	**Name and address**
2	**Checking and savings account numbers**
3	**Beginning and ending date for statement**
4	**Beginning balance**
5	**Total of all deposits**
6	**Total of all withdrawals**
7	**Ending balance**
8	**List of individual checks**
9	**ATM and debit card withdrawals**
10	**Customer service telephone number**
11	**Account balancing section**

Glossary

analyst person who examines something; a credit analyst looks over peoples credit applications

annual occurring or done every year

balance amount of money in an account; the act of checking an account against a bank statement

bank note piece of paper issued by a government-authorized bank and accepted as money

bankrupt legally unable to pay one's debts due to lack of money

borrower person who takes or receives something, like money, with the promise of returning it

circulation movement of currency from person to person or from place to place

communist describing a system with an economy planned and controlled by the state

counterfeit made as a false copy of something, especially money, with the intent to defraud or cheat someone

currency money in circulation

debt something that is owed

deposit to put in, as money into a bank account, or the amount put in

dominate to control by superior power

economy use or management of money

enforce to make others obey, as a rule or law

federal describing a union of states that share a government

financial relating to the management of money

financial institution company that deals with the management of money

fraud lies or trickery done to cheat someone

funds money

good thing that can be bought or sold

industrial relating to the manufacture of goods

interest amount charged for the right to use or borrow money

invest to contribute money to something in order to make a profit

investment act of putting money into a business in order to earn interest or profit

Islam religion that follows Allah as the one god and Muhammad as his prophet. Believers of Islam are called Muslims.

loan money given to a borrower, to be repaid with interest

merchant person who buys goods in one place and sells them in another, often a different country

microcredit very small amount, used to describe a small loan

minimum least possible amount

monetary having to do with money

mortgage money given to a person to buy a house or other piece of real estate with the understanding that it will be paid back with interest

penalty punishment for breaking a rule; in banking, usually involves paying a fee

profit money made in a business venture

repossess to take possession of again

Revolutionary War war fought from 1775 to 1783 between the British army and American colonists for control of the thirteen colonies

service work done for another or others

Social Security government program of retirement benefits

swipe to slide with a sweeping movement

terminal keyboard and video display that acts as a connection to a computer

transaction act of conducting business

transfer to move from one place to another

withdraw to remove, such as money from a bank account

More Books to Read

Burkett, Larry (ed.). *Money Matters for Kids.* Chicago: Moody Press, 2001.

Macht, Norman. *Money and Banking.* Broomall, Penn.: Chelsea House, 2001.

Simpson, Carolyn. *Choosing a Career in Banking and Finance.* New York: Rosen Publishing Group, 1999.

Learn about the banks in your community. Gather the booklets each bank hands out for free. Find the information you would need to choose a bank for a checking account. You may want to place the information in a table. This will make the information easier to compare.

Index